Wisdom-Driven Business

Wisdom-Driven Business

Carolyn Thurston

Wisdom Business Owner, LLC
Durham, NC

Wisdom-Driven Business
by Carolyn Thurston
Published 2025 by Wisdom Business Owner, LLC
Durham, NC 27707
Wisdomseniorcare.com

©2025 by Carolyn Thurston
All rights reserved. No part of this book may be reproduced or transmitted in any form whatsoever without permission from the author except in the case of brief quotations embodied in articles, reviews, or books.

First Edition Published by Wisdom Business Owner, LLC

Printed in the United States of America
1 2 3 4 5 6 7 8 9 0

ISBN-13: 979-8-9935792-0-7
e-ISBN: 979-8-9935792-1-4

Library of Congress Control Number: 2025922539

Editor: Ayanna Moo-Young

I dedicate this book to the Word of God which continues to lead and guide me as I complete my purpose in life, and to all those who have a dream inside and have been struggling to take a step forward.

Contents

Preface i

Introduction: Choosing Wisdom 1

Aligning with Your Purpose 5

Developing Confidence 11

Standing Firm 19

Building a Business Mindset 33

Doing One Thing Now 41

Understanding Business 47

Learning Lessons the First Time 63

Prioritizing Family 73

Avoiding Burnout 79

Scaling 85

Discovering Wisdom Today 93

Forgiving 97

Acknowledgements 101

About the Author 103

References 107

Preface

Pursuing your purpose is a decision. And embarking upon the journey of discovering who you are meant to become, combined with the intention of thriving as a successful business owner, involves learning to make the wisest choices. It involves being in alignment with what you've been called to do, learning not only about your craft and the product or service you intend to sell, but how to become business savvy. Gaining not only crucial business management skills but understanding how to create a sustainable business.

Sustainability involves openness to consistent education and evolution. Learning not only by trial and error or your own mistakes and successes, but from the blunders and victories of others will enable you to avoid pitfalls and apply meaningful strategies along the way. Most often, the roadmap to success has already been developed, learning *the hard way* or reinventing the wheel is unnecessary.

In *Wisdom-Driven Business,* Carolyn Thurston shares the story of personal challenges and triumphs she has experienced in pursuit of her purpose and passion. Carolyn inspires others not to give up on finding and living their purpose while revealing risks to avoid. And anyone who is contemplating using their purpose to build a business, startups as well as those who are looking to sharpen their skills as established business owners, will glean invaluable knowledge on the character traits and skills required to yield positive results. Prepare to become inspired. Lead with action.

Introduction: Choosing Wisdom

"If any of you lacks wisdom, let him ask God, who gives generously to all without reproach, and it will be given him." James 1:5

Make wise decisions. Make smart choices. These are commands that we've all heard from those who have cared for us throughout our lifetimes. Many of us can recall these words being spoken to us as children, echoing throughout the rooms of our homes during family discussions and saturating the fabric of the seats in our family vehicles during long road trips.

These words stuck with us. They permeated through our hearts and minds during times when we were separated from our parents while at school, hanging out with friends, or at sporting events. Other adults – our grandparents, guardians, mentors, bosses, and others who have shaped and molded us – offered similar advice and warnings. During Sunday school sessions, our Sunday school teachers spoon-fed us biblical verses containing the word *wisdom* and warned us of the consequences if we did not adhere to the Word of God.

When we were faced with moments of tough challenge and temptation, we sometimes conformed to the behaviors that were deemed acceptable and wise. At other times, we did not. When we faltered, because we were taught that wisdom was more of a theoretical concept, a religious undertaking, and/or something developed from decades of experience, we doubted ourselves. And we chalked our behaviors up to inexperience, ignorance, and mismanagement of our impulses. Some of us might've absorbed feelings of guilt, shame, and helplessness for not following the script developed for us by our authority figures. But those same figures taught us through the years that wisdom comes from experience. In fact, Job 12:12 asks the questions: *"Is not wisdom found among the aged? Does not long life bring understanding?"*

Introduction: Choosing Wisdom

However, if we were to examine wisdom from a much broader perspective, we'd understand it as a multifaceted concept. We'd acknowledge that there are multiple ways to become wise and there are many areas of our lives for which we should develop wisdom.

Some people are wise when it comes to making decisions about the company they keep but may not make wise choices when it comes to workplace etiquette. Some people have the most wisdom in the areas of communication and relationships, but don't make the wisest health decisions. Some people are very streetwise but make unwise financial decisions. And the list goes on.

Yes, we gain wisdom from our own experiences; we gain new experiences with each passing day that we live. The older we become the more experiences we'll have. But we can also gain wisdom through education and the experiences of others. We can gain wisdom through exploration and research. We can become wiser by examining other cultures and embracing the differences of others. And when you start a business, life's lessons, education, exploratory adventures, and connectedness all come to a head. We need them all to achieve great levels of success.

Aligning with Your Purpose

---

*"Trust in the Lord with all your heart,
and do not lean on your own
understanding. In all your ways
acknowledge Him, and He will direct
your paths." Proverbs 3:5-6*

We all have a purpose. It usually lies within those things that we are most passionate about. It's the one thing that drives us to feel energized and motivated over anything else. Perhaps we are most in tune with it as children because we are fearless; but, somehow, when we become adults, we lose touch with it. But passion and purpose never leave us. They lie dormant waiting for us to act.

Our purpose is something that no one can take from us; yet, for many people it often goes unfulfilled. Are you currently involved in the industry or position that is tied to your life's purpose? Dream lifestyle? If your response is *no*, you're not alone. Most people will never pursue their purpose. There are several reasons they will not.

One of the main reasons people are afraid is that others will judge them. No matter our age, our appearances, or our socio-economic statuses, we are all vulnerable to what our peers think of us. And without a firm foundation built with faith, we are susceptible to their criticisms. Whether it's our parents, siblings, trusted friends, a colleague, or a mentor, once we've folded to the opinions of others, we have granted them power over our decisions. Conceding to one decision that is most important to us invites additional unwelcome impositions.

Some people have tried to fulfill a purpose or a goal but quit after the first sign of failure. These people don't see failure as a lesson, so they don't understand what they could've possibly learned from the experience. They are so focused on the end result that they forget that achieving success in anything involves a process. They may even feel embarrassed that their plans didn't work out for them the first time, consciously remembering that the onlookers have been watching. They'd prefer to be misunderstood by their peers and the people they care most about than to be wrong. Instead of giving it another try, they fall back into mediocrity. They wake up each morning and prepare for the job they hate, settling for short-term rewards, imagining what could have been if that one attempt had produced immediate gratification. Some stop believing in themselves altogether.

Other people want to pursue their purpose, but they lack self-discipline. While motivation can be fleeting, self-discipline is sustainable. Self-discipline is preparation. It is about planning routines around your goals and executing them. It is the ultimate test of the will against distractions. It is about doing what is required when you should, even when you don't feel like it.

Your purpose is the reason you believe you exist in this world. It involves what your higher power has called you to do. It is something to be attained, something to aspire towards. To pursue and fulfill it, you must align with it. Know it deeply. Believe you deserve to achieve it. Commit to it.

What is your purpose? What do you believe you have been put on this earth to accomplish? What has been carved out just for you?

If you have yet to discover your purpose, one way to get closer to confirmation is to reflect on which activities in your life excite you and leave you feeling most fulfilled and accomplished. Do you have a special talent, skill, or hobby that you would feel lost without? What are your core values and how does the thing that you're passionate about factor into them? What career opportunities have you accepted in the past and which of them made you feel most purposeful? If you could create a business opportunity with your passion as the anchor, would you? Allow God to guide you. Use the inner voice and intuition He has provided as support.

Aligning with Your Purpose

Exploring your purpose doesn't just stop at doing what you're passionate about, also consider the things that you're actually good at. These are your strengths. Some people are excellent communicators while others are better at solving technical problems in a silo. Some are wonderful designers while others are better suited modeling designs made specifically for them. What are the strong characteristics you possess that come natural to you? When identifying your purpose, consider them.

Another often overlooked detail to consider when aligning with your purpose is the legacy you'd like to leave behind. Your legacy extends far beyond the assets you'd like to leave for your beneficiaries. It's also about impact. The lasting blueprints, imprints, and footprints that are left once you're gone. These are the paths and innovations you've created, the lasting impressions you've made, and the mistakes and successes you've produced that are left for others to learn from. What do you most want to be remembered for? The business you create around your purpose should include these ideas.

There is no guaranteed path to successfully finding your purpose, operating in it, and making a real impact. However, if you want to be more than average, you must be willing to do extraordinary things in life. Break the barriers to your success. Dare to be different; do what others won't. Own your peculiarities and allow others to criticize and ridicule you without turning back. Allow the seeds of possibility and belief to take root in your garden. Create and live your ideal future on purpose.

Developing Confidence

---

*"A man's wisdom makes his face
shine, and the hardness of his
countenance is changed."*
Ecclesiastes 8:1

Confidence is a personality trait that most of us are not born with but can be developed over time. It is rooted in belief in yourself, your capabilities and self-worth. It is an important aspect of gaining the courage to step out of your comfort zone and address fear.

I have learned over the years how important it is to have confidence in myself despite the opinions of others. I knew that if I did not believe in myself, the ability to accomplish my dreams would become more challenging. Self-confidence was instilled in me by my parents at an early age.

As a child, I had the opportunity to travel with my family because my father was in the United States

Air Force. I found traveling exciting because moving to a new place gave me the opportunity to start over; but on the other hand, I became shy. I was always the new person in class and never knew whether people would like me or would want to get to know me. I didn't want them to judge me; this was a deep concern. I learned to wait and observe how people responded to me before speaking to them.

I can remember doubting myself as far back as the age of 5. At this time, my father was in the United States Air Force, stationed at Buck Harbor in Maine. I was in the first grade and didn't feel adequate.

Maine was a cold, snowy place. We ate lunch in our classrooms. The feeling I had on the first day of class sticks with me to this day. Whenever I arrived at a new school, teachers would always ask me to come to the front of the class, to share my name and where I came from. This school was no different. When the teacher asked me to introduce myself, a great fear hit me in the pit of my stomach. I felt that the other students already knew each other and would not want me to join them at their tables. I realized after a couple of weeks this was not the case. I met at least one friend who took me under their wing. During this time, I would not look a person in the eye, believing they would be able to see who I was and decide not to like me. It is interesting to look back and wonder why I thought I wouldn't make friends. I was a kind child, not a bully, who had empathy for others. I possessed a keen instinct to feel the pain I assumed others felt when faced with a tough situation.

We all experience self-doubt at some point in our lives. It must be dealt with. A key to conquering it is to first recognize it; raise your self-awareness. And once you've identified it, it can best be used to your advantage to help drive growth and change.

I somehow intuitively knew that one of my biggest challenges was self-doubt and I resolved to find solutions. When I was in high school, whenever I went to the library to check out books, I was drawn to the self-improvement section. I recognized at the age of 15 that I needed to improve myself to become successful.

Why would I think self-improvement would lead to success? What was my definition of success at age 15? Money. My definition of success during those times was connected to how much money was in my purse.

I sought the advice of my guidance counselor who suggested that I participate in the school drama department to help address my shy nature. My father did not like the idea, it upset him. However, every morning before the beginning of our school day, we said the pledge of allegiance and broadcast the morning announcements over the loudspeaker. I enjoyed this process because it meant that people were not watching me and could only hear my voice; I was more at ease.

My brother was a football player, and I enjoyed watching the cheerleaders perform. I even dreamt of one day becoming a cheerleader. I daydreamed and imagined myself becoming either a cheerleader or an actress. I would practice for hours in our kitchen after dinner and during clean up rehearsed cheers that I had seen others perform. I also practiced for plays but when the time came, I would not have the confidence to perform.

    My first year in high school we were stationed in England. I gained enough confidence to try out for the cheerleading squad and was so excited and confident. I went out on the stage in the high school auditorium as 6 judges scored the performances. We each had to perform a cheer and received our results the next day. They put all who had made varsity on the window of the auditorium. I looked down at the list and saw my name. My mother states this was the happiest she had ever seen me; I had practiced so long for that day. My confidence started to increase due to this victory. I even became head cheerleader the following year, but I was not psychologically ready to endure the obstacles of a leader.

I did not realize that there was a girl who wanted the captain's position until after I became the head cheerleader. And one day when I arrived at our routine practice, I was notified that I would no longer be the head cheerleader. I had been secretly voted out of the position.

I was truly devastated. Worse, all the people I had confidence in turned their backs on me, stating there was nothing they could do. My heart was broken. I could not believe people could be so devious, and I knew in my gut that this was wrong. I researched who to speak with and requested the rules concerning the process, only to succumb to what had happened.

Through this experience, God was preparing me for a key business lesson: to know and understand the true intentions of others before collaboration begins. Someone lurking in the shadows holds the belief that they are a better fit for your position. They will come for it, given the right space, time, and opportunity.

Developing Confidence

After that experience, I made a promise to myself that I would never allow anyone to do this to me again. My supportive network, my family, encouraged me and assisted me through this process. However, this planted a seed of doubt in my leadership ability. This was my first encounter with a person who had set out to destroy my confidence, but it wouldn't be the last. But the confidence that I developed throughout those years is what has aided me during my toughest moments both in my personal life and in business.

My definition of success has evolved with maturity. Today, I perceive success as joy, happiness, health, and internal peace. Internal peace is my indicator that I'm doing what is required and moving in the right direction. I ask myself: *How many people are better off since we met?*

I've also learned not to be so hasty to compare myself to others. When I need a reminder, I remember the Word of God's description of how I was made. I am made in God's image! Let's think about that … Image is not only external but internal, emotional, and biological. This revelation now assists me in dealing with self-doubt when it raises its ugly head. Affirming this level of self-confidence is what sparked my true path ablaze. And I would not allow anyone to quench the fire.

Standing Firm

---

*"Wisdom is the principal thing;
therefore get wisdom; and with all they
getting get understanding." Proverbs
4:7*

I eagerly awaited an appointment with my guidance counselor in a chair situated right outside her office. It was my eleventh-grade year – the year we were expected to choose our career paths and decide whether to apply to colleges or trade school or enter the workforce. I hadn't been the best student. My grades were average at best; I had struggled in many subjects in which my peers seemed to excel. College and career options were something that I carefully took time to ponder. I knew that I wanted to do something meaningful, but it took some time for me to discover my true passion.

On this day, I had a clear thought and intention of where I was headed in life. As I sat consumed with anticipation, I watched and listened to the hustle and bustle of the guidance suite – the ringing of the analog telephone, the heavy, wooden door opening and closing as students entered and exited through the reception area, the occasional interruption over the loudspeaker from the main office requesting support for a student.

The well-lit reception area was one typical of most high schools. Hand-made posters announcing upcoming elections for the prom king and queen alongside banners warning students of the dangers of drugs and alcohol abuse. College literature was displayed on a resource table near the blue and green cushioned seats occupied by students waiting for their names to be called. It was a busy time of year. We juniors were focused on planning our futures. And the seniors? Their last-ditch efforts to ensure they had enough credits to walk across the stage at graduation.

Standing Firm

I sat confidently, proudly, and patiently. Neatly dressed in one of my favorite red plaid skirts, a white button-down collared shirt, white, ruffled socks, and black patent leather shoes. My hair laid backward and captured in the usual ponytail, and my ears adorned with my favorite small, gold hoops.

The aroma of possibility and promise saturated the air. I knew exactly what I wanted to do with my life, and I was ecstatic about sharing the plan with my guidance counselor. Today's goal was to discuss the plan in detail and strategize the next steps toward implementation.

Finally, her office door flung open, and a student exited through the entry way; it was finally my turn. "Carolyn, come on in," she instructed, warmly inviting me to have a seat across from her desk.

As we sat, she reviewed my transcript and reiterated that the purpose of our meeting was to discuss my plans after high school. I smiled and shared, "I've thought about it quite extensively; I would really like to attend nursing school. I want to become a nurse!"

She paused and stared at me for a moment. Then, she replied, "Carolyn, let's be realistic. Why don't you become a secretary instead?"

***

Who has the authority to make your life's decisions? Many people who place their dreams on pause or don't make an effort to achieve them at all are afraid of judgment. They have granted others power over their life decisions. Think about it: how often has someone else – a cousin, a teacher, a parent, a sibling, a colleague, or a friend – tried to convince you that your ideas were outlandish? That you need to get your head out of the clouds and grow up? That your small mind isn't equipped for that big role?

Others see you through their own lenses, the perspectives and biases they've developed based on their experiences, and the fear they've developed as a result. And what do we do? We quit. We allow the dream to fester, to eat away at our minds and we share with others later in life what we should've or would've accomplished had we had the courage, the opportunity, or the resources. I was determined that this would not be my fate. I wouldn't allow my counselor's opinion of my abilities to stop me from forging ahead. Nursing was a career that was placed in my heart by God. And what God has already affirmed, no man can deny.

"No, I will be a nurse." These were my exact words to my guidance counselor after she attempted to persuade me that nursing was not my calling. It did not matter to me that I had a C- grade point average. I was not going to allow her to dictate my future. God had not only given me the idea, but the seed had already been planted in my heart and began to germinate. And if I was going to be bold enough to obey the vision God had given me, I had no choice but to become a nurse. This didn't mean that I wasn't fearful. It meant that I was willing to push past any inner resistance to make it a reality. This desire within me was so strong that I could not give up, I had to keep trying until something happened.

I could've left my counselor's office that day feeling afraid, defeated, or discouraged; but I didn't. Instead, I felt empowered. Her lack of support and encouragement turned a flicker of hope into a flame of determination. She didn't have to believe in me. She did not have to see the vision; it was mine to see, not hers. I don't believe she had malice intent; she had reduced herself to a perception of my capabilities based on *her* truths, backed by *her* knowledge and experience. I knew better. I simply didn't accept her perceptions of truth as my own.

I arrived home that evening on a mission. I entered the foyer area and removed my shoes. Mom was waiting for me with the usual questions: *"How was school? Anything interesting?"* to which I responded my usual, "It was fine." I wasn't ready to share more. I needed space. I was laser focused.

I jetted upstairs to my bedroom. I reached for the stack of applications for colleges across the eastern United States I had begun accumulating earlier in the year. I homed in, putting pen to paper. I then applied to more colleges than I'd like to admit, using earnings that I had saved from babysitting gigs to afford the application fees. A few weeks later, I began anticipating acceptance letters in the mail. I knew that I would not be accepted into them all, but surely, I met the qualifications for some.

The decision letters finally began rolling in – *Declined acceptance…We regret to inform you that …Try again…Application denied.* The negative responses were overwhelming. Denial letters became so familiar that they were embedded into the evening routine: coming home from school, having a snack, and reading yet another denial letter.

Doubt began to surface. How was I going to become a nurse if college was not in my future? Then finally, I received an acceptance letter; not one that I wanted but one that I needed. I accepted enrollment in the University of Maryland's extension program.

The University of Maryland offers a program for graduating seniors who are looking to explore college life experience and enroll in college-level courses. At the time, I was still living in England. The University had a footprint there. Accepting The University of Maryland's offer to attend their extension program enabled me to begin taking college courses, and I continued this path until I had accomplished enough credit hours to apply to a university. I also did not want to take a long break or enter the workforce directly after graduation, and I believed that my participation in the program would get me one step closer to full-time enrollment at a college or university of my choice.

I began with beginner level courses in communications and speech. This boosted my confidence; I excelled tremendously. My grades were the best I had ever achieved. This success served as proof to my parents and I that I could thrive in a college setting.

I built the courage to apply to North Carolina Central University's nursing program. When I received their response in the mail, I had no doubt. I wasn't nervous at all because I already knew that the answer was yes; I was accepted. This was such a joyful day. I had achieved my desire to get into college, hence placing myself on the path to becoming a registered nurse. My participation in the ROTC program at school had fueled my desire to become a nurse officer in the military. So, the journey towards my purpose began.

During my first semester in 1986, I was also introduced to a young man named Charles Thurston, a student at Hampton University. As the story goes, Charles's mother was concerned that he was bringing home the type of women who did not live up to her standards. I was living with my grandfather, and Charles had an aunt, who lived next door, informed his mother, Mrs. Thurston, that she believed I was a well-mannered, intelligent, wholesome girl who would be a positive influence on Charles.

Charles's mother was an outspoken woman who did not waste time. She called me with a request: "Will you come down to our house so we can meet you?" I agreed.

When the day arrived, Charles picked me up from my grandfather's house and we drove to his house where both his parents waited. After a round of small talk followed by more pointed questions, I earned their approval. Charles and I began to date. I was now completing coursework and dating a wonderful guy; I was ecstatic.

However, as they often did during those times, another challenge arose. I knew that to remain in the nursing program at North Carolina Central, I needed to maintain a 3.0 GPA. I did not meet my obligation. I was forced to decide between two options: quit or change my major.

Nursing was a passion of mine and aligned with my purpose. Nothing was going to stop me.

Despite the naysayers, the denial letters, the small fortune spent on getting one step closer to making my dream a reality, I had made a commitment to myself not to give up. And when God places something in your heart and you act, it will not be denied. His answers are *Yes and Amen.* If there wasn't a door open for me in the nursing profession, I would create one. I had researched and contemplated which majors would complement nursing and afford an opportunity to gain experience helping others. Sociology.

But even after earning a Bachelor of Arts in Sociology, the desire to become a registered nurse continued to burn inside of me. I envisioned myself wearing a nurse's uniform, commuting to work at a hospital, and working with patients. This was the painting I had carefully stroked in my heart and couldn't let go of. Using a phonebook, I conducted a search for nursing schools, which led me to call Winston Salem State University.

During a telephone call with a kind woman in the nursing department, I was notified that I qualified to attend their nursing program. Faith and hope that I could still become a registered nurse increased, and I decided that it was best to complete the program than to allow another 2 years to go by and wish that I had.

"You don't know anyone in Winston Salem; where will you stay?" My family wondered. However, my faith was so strong that I was unable to see any obstacles. I kept pressing forward which led me to a room for rent advertisement on campus. When I called, the woman mentioned that the advertisement was old but instructed me to stop by because she believed I was nice, and she wanted to meet me in person. I accepted her request, and not only did I gain a place to stay; we also developed a lasting friendship.

We have control over our fears, not the other way around. Think about it: fear is the appearance of something being real. What frightens us most can only become reality if we attach meaning to it.

Perfectionism is a form of fear. Those of us who await the perfect opportunity, conditions, or timing are truly fearful. Because I've personally struggled with indecisiveness and analysis paralysis throughout my lifetime, those close to me have dubbed me a perfectionist.

When I imagine a perfectionist, the vision looks nothing like me. I picture a perfectionist as someone who has every hair on their head intact, someone who ensures every *I* is dotted, and *T* is crossed, and someone who is extra critical of others. I'm not that way at all.

But another aspect of perfectionism is the fear that you're going to get it wrong, that everything must unfold as planned. And my inability to stop analyzing and make quick, sound decisions have at times led to delayed progress and cloudy judgment. Be conscious of these tendencies. Fear is one of our biggest enemies which could lead to both mental and physical illnesses that not only affect us, but those closest to our hearts.

The summer of 1992 was full of amazing life events. I graduated with honors from Winston Salem State University's School of Nursing. I passed the board of nursing exams and began a new job as a registered nurse. And after dating for 7.5 years, Charles and I got married. If I had quit, I wouldn't have experienced all the goodness God had in store for me that year. Standing firm on what He promised is what got me there.

Building a Business Mindset

"The fear of the Lord is the beginning of wisdom, and knowledge of the Holy One is understanding." Proverbs 9:10

In the business world, the term *business minded* is often used loosely, but what does it truly mean? It involves the development of mental habits that help maximize success. These habits include creating priorities, making decisions based on your mission and vision, taking calculated risks, being action-oriented, using your time effectively, and the list goes on. Let's face it, there are many business owners who have yet to master this set of skills, and it could be especially difficult for those who have transitioned from being an employee at someone else's company. The fact that you are responsible for the decisions that you make, whether they lead to success or failure, is one of the best benefits and challenges of going into business.

You must think and behave like a business owner. Follow the correct path. Head in a clear direction with your goals. Maintain a positive outlook. This is key. Your faith must be stronger than your fears, you must begin to view obstacles as opportunities and be willing to evolve personally and professionally. Doing so will enable you to develop enough competence and confidence to be successful.

The greatest obstacles are fear and self-doubt, but building competence and confidence will help to mitigate them along the way. While it's never too late, it's best to develop a business state of mind and habits before opening the doors.

Explore your current mindset and behavioral patterns. What are your habits? Which could help you prosper in business, and which could impede your progress? You already know the difference between the two. The most uplifting habits are the ones that make you feel productive when you are engaged with them. They result in outcomes that make you feel great about yourself and your accomplishments. The unproductive habits are the ones that leave you feeling unaccomplished, stuck, and guilty.

Successful business owners abide by key principles and practices that enable them to maintain a business mindset. We've already addressed one of the most important foundational steps which is determining your purpose, your *why*, for going into business in the first place. Always keep this at the forefront. But there are other important measures to consider that will assist you in attaining and maintaining success. Think like the gurus.

After you've determined your purpose, create a vision. You must be able to imagine where you want your business to be in the future and begin to work towards that mental image. Along with your why, your vision is an essential component that will help you to maintain clarity and focus. Remember, creating a vision is not about knowing all the steps on how to achieve it, it's about understanding where you aspire to be in the coming years. What is the ultimate goal you'd like to achieve? What does the major problem that you're solving look like once it's resolved? When your target market has benefited from your solution, how do they look, behave, and feel?

Create a vision in your mind. Thinking of the end goal, how will your product or service add value to your customers? In what ways has your offer benefited them? If you noticed, I did not ask you straight away how much money you'd like to make. Although we all want a profitable business, money should not be your greatest motivator. How you'll make a difference is much more important; it is your mission and vision. And although the mission and vision can change overtime, your purpose is the one thing that typically remains constant.

Another crucial factor is goal setting. Setting goals enables you to design a clear path towards achieving your mission and vision. There are many goal-setting strategies that have been developed by experts over the years. One of them that I find simplest to remember and implement is the SMART

Goals method. SMART Goals are specific, measurable, achievable, relevant, and time bound.

Be specific with your goals. What are the short-term and long-term goals that will put you in position to attain your mission and vision statements? I've found it most useful to keep stated goals as clear and concise as possible without being too broad. Be as specific with your goals as you are when describing your dream car. When you write down information on the dream car you'd like to purchase, you wouldn't simply note the make of the vehicle. You'd also list the model, exterior color, interior color, technology features, and so on.

How will you know when you have achieved the goal? You must determine methods for measuring success. Will you use qualitative or quantitative data or both? Think about which instruments or software you will utilize to keep track of progress.

Ensure that your goals are achievable and relevant. You'll want to set yourself up to achieve small successes. Avoid setting unrealistic bars that will set you and your team up for failure. If you had ten customers at the beginning of the week, you wouldn't set a goal of achieving one million customers by week's end. And be certain that the goals you're setting suit your specific business, the products and services that you offer, and the business model.

When will the goal be accomplished? What is the timeframe? Three days? Six months? One year? Be sure to write it down. Create check-in points to monitor your progress and make adjustments as needed.

Another mindset characteristic that business gurus have in common is that they never stop learning; they've adopted a growth mindset. They not only learn from mistakes, but they stay abreast of industry practices including technological advances. Success is earned each day. Today's success does not secure tomorrow's future unless we are willing to learn and adapt to change. Stay ahead of the curve to seize the future of your business. Complacency could cost you your company. This fact has been proven repeatedly throughout history.

Build strong relationships with your team, your customers, and your colleagues. Success is driven by relationships. Not how smart you are. Not by how much money you have in the bank. Not by desire alone. Relationships. Build meaningful ones. Know how to lead your team by example, when to delegate and build other leaders, and how to remind them every day how important they and their contributions are to you and to the success of the organization. Understand your customers by consistently listening to their feedback and creating opportunities to reward those who are loyal. Connect with your colleagues by creating reciprocal and rewarding relationships where you can support and learn from one another.

There are many other factors that play a role in building a business mindset, but I'll share one last, principal factor that I'll continue reiterating. Not every goal will be accomplished when and how you'd like, not every person you believe to be an ally will prove to be so, not every dollar you've allocated to grow your business is assured to be spent how you planned. Business can be unpredictable at times, but it is worth it. Be resilient. Remember why you started, connect with like-minded people, build mental fortitude, and stay the course. And when you start to experience even the smallest wins, celebrate.

These are some of the greatest factors in running a business. They will enable you to remain focused and make decisions that are aligned with your goals. Keeping them at the forefront will also enable you to stay encouraged when you are thrown a curveball or are confronted by a naysayer. Both are inevitable.

Doing One Thing Now

"If you are wise and understand God's ways prove it by living an honorable life, doing good works with the humility that comes from wisdom." James 3:13

By December of 2005, I was ready to make a change. I had been working as director of operations for a home health company in North Carolina at the time. Although I had poured all that I had into making this company grow: hiring staff, obtaining contracts, working all day, bringing work home, etc., it seemed that I'd never meet the objectives of the corporate team. I knew that my faith in God would lead me and provide the resources required to complete the tasks at hand, but I felt unappreciated and found myself relying on my own skills and abilities instead of allowing God to be in control fully.

My two girls were small. I would bathe and clothe them, put them to bed, then stay up working to ensure all processes were followed. I eventually concluded that I needed to do something different if I wanted something different. I now believe that what I perceived as an obstacle was God guiding me into the direction He needed me to go to arrive at His purpose for my life.

One night, I asked myself: "What can I do right now?" This was a powerful question that required a change in thinking. I needed to focus on what I had at my disposal instead of the laundry list of things I did not have. Suddenly, the one thing I could do at that moment came into my awareness. I learned that I had enough time and money to complete a North Carolina home care license application. This was step that I initially would not move towards; I assumed that I would not be able to afford it and that the application itself was cumbersome. I had made this up; it was only an assumption. I had yet to complete any research.

Doing One Thing Now

By taking the first step and researching the requirements, I learned that the application fee was only $300.00; I could afford that! So, I completed the application and awaited the next steps. I was overcome with both excitement and uncertainty, but I knew I was finally moving in faith with what God had told me back in 1982 while I was still in high school – that I would start my own business and its name would be *Wisdom*.

In February of 2006, I became a licensed home care provider in the State of North Carolina and Wisdom Healthcare Solutions was launched as a service-based business. My first client, a dog.

***

What can you do right now to get one step closer? For me, it was the uncomplicated process of completing an application and paying a fee. For you, it could be something even simpler. Think about it, especially if you have yet to take any steps at all. It's time to stop overanalyzing and complaining about what you do not have at your disposal, and to begin thinking about what you do have, and what you can do. There's always a step, a baby step or a gigantic leap, which can be completed today. Choose one thing and begin to build upon it.

In the book *The ONE Thing*, authors Gary Keller and Jay Papsan offer a compelling perspective on how people can complete important tasks while reducing clutter and distractions. The premise of the book lies in one question: *"What's the one thing I can do right now such that by doing it everything else will be easier or unnecessary?"* Consider asking yourself this question when completing everyday tasks, and I suggest that you also apply it to your desire to start and scale your business.

If your industry requires licensure, what do you need to do to obtain it? If you are considering a brick-and-mortar business, have you scouted the best locations and analyzed the acquisition costs? If you're like me and have a desire to make a difference changing lives in the healthcare industry, whose life would you like to enhance and in what ways? What does scaling your business look like and what are the first steps? After asking yourself this series of questions and researching their responses, focus on a step that is significant enough to propel you forward. Then, actually do it.

You may want a million dollars, but is that amount of money necessary to take the first step? Remember, even some of the biggest businesses that we know today started with an idea and humble beginnings.

Tech giant Hewlett Packard first began as an electronics company. Its initial startup cost was $538. Its first office? A garage. Today, the company employs more than 60,000 people and rakes in an annual net revenue of $63 billion.

Understanding Business

"Wisdom is the principal thing; therefore get wisdom; and with all they getting get understanding." Proverbs 4:7

The more competent you become about your business, the more confidence you'll generate. As a confident business owner, you'll catapult your business into many successful experiences. To achieve this, you must take the first steps. Become educated not only in your craft, but in general business principles such as leadership, business management, financial planning and management, communications, and problem solving, to name a few. You'll want to learn more about your target market and how to generate fresh, innovative ideas. You'll need to know how to win customers and how to retain them. Most importantly, you must learn about yourself. You must be aware of the internal barriers you've created throughout the years that could hinder your business and personal growth. Follow these three rules:

1. Learn everything there is to know about the product or service you intend to offer. What are the best practices? Is your idea needed in the marketplace? How much will you charge for your product or service? How will you remain relevant to your customers?

2. Learn the fundamental steps to starting a business the right way. Which business structure best suits you? What are the startup costs? Where will you incorporate? Where will you open your first bank account?

3. Know thyself. What childhood traumas have been left unresolved? What unproductive habits have been a hindrance to your progress? In what ways will you work to improve yourself daily?

Deciding the best business structure and model for your business is essential. Once you know the product or service you'd like to offer and who your customers are, you'll need to understand the best business structure for your situation and how to bring your ideas to market.

Business Structures

A business structure is the legal framework for how a business is organized, operated, and owned. It informs decisions such as liability, taxation, and reporting requirements. Some common business structures include limited liability companies (LLCs), S-corps, C-corps, and nonprofit organizations. Choosing the right structure is essential and, unfortunately, many business owners are not well-educated on the different structures and may default to one type over the other out of ignorance. Doing so could inhibit your business's ability to grow and thrive. You may start by educating yourself on the basics. Here are more details about each structure:

Limited Liability Company (LLC)

A limited liability company offers protections for your personal assets such as your house, car, and bank accounts, should your business ever be faced with bankruptcy or lawsuits. The business's profits and losses are typically reported on your personal tax returns unless you opt to be taxed as a corporation with the IRS. The tax rate for an LLC is usually lower than corporations.

C-Corp

A C-Corp, or corporation, is an entity that is separated from its owners and offers the strongest personal liability protection because the business itself is held liable for taxes and legal obligations. C-Corps have the ability to go public, raise money, and secure additional shareholders who will have a stake in the company. This business structure can be doubly taxed on both profits and dividends.

S-Corp

An S-Corp is a special corporation that enables the company to avoid the double taxation of a C-Corp. This business structure enables the owners to pass through some of the business's profits and losses on their personal returns. The number of shareholders is limited. However, some states don't recognize this structure. It is important to understand the laws in the state where you intend to incorporate your business entity to decide if this is the right structure for you.

Nonprofit Corporation

Charitable, educational, religious, literary, and scientific work is mainly organized through nonprofit corporations. Nonprofit entities do not pay federal or state taxes on the profits that they make, but they must be registered and approved to be considered tax exempt by both their state and the federal government to receive this benefit. They must also abide by rules regarding how to disperse profits, reporting requirements, and more.

Advised by a certified public accountant or CPA, I started Wisdom Healthcare Solutions as an S-Corp. It was the structure that made most sense for my business at the time. Remember, you don't have to know everything, and you don't have to make this major decision alone. There are attorneys, accountants, business consultants, etc. available to assist you. A true CPA will listen to your business idea and goals and will recommend the right structure for you.

Business Models

On the other hand, a business model dictates how a company's products or services are delivered and how the business earns a profit. There are over 50 business models. The most popular models that most business startups select include products, services, subscriptions, freemium, and franchise. While this list isn't exhaustive, many businesses fall into these categories.

Products

This model involves manufacturing and/or retailing items for profit.

Services

This model is centered around providing labor and services (i.e., home health care).

Subscription

This model requires on-going payment for a fixed duration in exchange for products or services.

Freemium

This model involves offering products or services at no cost that the business can leverage to charge a premium price for supplemental or advanced features.

Franchise

This model leverages an existing plan that enables the business to expand and reproduce at a different location.

Funding Your Business

One of the biggest fears of people who form business startups is how they will fund their operations. There are many options available to business owners, and each have their own criteria for qualification. They each also have their own upsides and nuances, and what is suitable for one business may not be suitable for the next. Each business owner is responsible for becoming educated about opportunities that are available to them to ensure that their business is sustainable and, eventually, scalable. Here are some common funding options to consider:

Business Loans

Whether secured through an online institution or a traditional brick and mortar bank, business loans are funds that are paid to the business with terms attached. These terms include the loan amount, when the loan will be paid back and how often, and the interest rate. Some lenders may place restrictions on how the funds can be used. Each institution that offers business loans has its own unique qualifications and payback terms, so it's best to cast a wide net when exploring options available to you.

Lines of Credit

You can apply for a line of credit through online sources or traditional banks. Again, each will have their own criterion. The main difference between a line of credit and a loan is that when you've been approved for a line of credit, you are only paying interest on the funds that you actually use. For example, if you've been awarded a $100,000 line of credit and you make a $20,000 purchase, you will pay interest on the $20,000. It's a flexible way to access funds when needed.

Investors

Investors typically offer business financing in exchange for equity in the company, interest on their money, or both. Navigating the world of investors can be complicated. There are distinct types of investors including venture capitalists, angel investors, and others, each having their own criterion for the industries they support, what they offer, and how you should present your business to them for consideration.

Crowd Funding

Crowd funding involves collecting small amounts of capital from a large number of people and is typically implemented at the startup phase of business. This type of funding has gained more popularity over recent years. Crowd funding can be equity-based, donation-based, reward-based, or debt-based. There are several online platforms that businesses use to raise capital through crowdfunding. GoFundMe, Indiegogo, and Kickstarter are examples.

Grants

Who wouldn't want free money? Essentially that is what grants are! Business grants are probably one of the most underutilized forms of business funding because many business owners don't know they exist or how to access them. Grants also come with stipulations. There may be strict qualifications, restrictions on how the funds are used, and monitoring requirements. The processing time to secure grant funding may be slower than most other forms of business funding.

Bootstrapping

Bootstrapping is when you fund your own business with your own money. Although many business owners who prefer this method are proud that they have the capital to fund their own businesses without taking on debt, using this method to fund your business could bring you to financial ruin and essentially cause your business to fail. I highly advise business owners to seek funding, access to lending, lines of credit, business credit cards, etc. as early in their business as possible. I did not begin Wisdom Healthcare Solutions that way.

I started Wisdom as a service-based company with what I had in my bank account or what is known as *bootstrapping*. If I had known better, I would not have funded the business this way. It is best to qualify the business for loans, lines of credit, etc. when you don't need the money than the need to scramble for funds in an emergency. If you initially learn that you don't qualify for capital, learn what you need to do to gain access. Not having it could slow your progress and make the journey unpleasant.

Connecting with Experts

None of us can do it all alone, not if we want to be successful. Seek to connect with not just one individual, but a team. This success strategy has been valuable to me. After finding experts for key elements of my business, I realized if I was going to continue to grow, I needed an advisory board. Having experts in one place focusing on you and your business is a revolutionary experience. I've gained a wealth of knowledge, and I've avoided many mistakes by using my advisory board as a sounding board. Doing so not only provided me with knowledge, but it offered an additional layer of protection. Remember, there is safety in numbers.

Experts come in all forms. Some are the unpaid mentors that cross our paths along the way, offering sound advice. Another resource is the Small Business Administration where you can enroll into several programs designed to connect you with experienced business owners who can support you. Other resources include paid mentors, advisors, and coaches that have created programs and platforms to share their experiences and expertise with others.

You'll find immense value in networking if you're strategic and purposeful. Whether you've crossed paths with someone and believe that you could add value to one another in some way or you've attended a massive networking event, you must know how to weed out people who will not take your goals seriously and will waste your time. Go in with a plan. Who are you interested in meeting? What value are you going to add to the conversation first? How and when will you follow up? Many people attend networking events and never follow up. Always follow up in 24-48 hours.

Connect with industry gurus – those with advanced knowledge and skills in your business. Attend their speaking events and subscribe to their online platforms. What practices have made them most successful?

Continuing Education

To be a great steward of your business, you must be a life-long learner. The degrees and licenses that you acquired in the beginning are not enough. To stay relevant and innovative, and to ensure that you are offering your customers the best services and keeping up with the latest technological advances in your industry, you must educate yourself.

Stay abreast of industry practices; attend conferences, webinars, and workshops. Listen to podcasts and watch videos that offer beneficial information that will help you sharpen your skills. Seek additional certifications and licensure when available or go back to school and enter a degree program in your field. Lean on advisors and mentors for the answers; ask questions. And most importantly, learn from mistakes. Your mistakes and the mistakes of those who have come before you.

Passion is not enough to experience success. Take a basic business course. Although passion will drive you toward the mark, basic knowledge of business is paramount. Powering the two together will make you unstoppable.

Learning Lessons the First Time

"The fear of the Lord is the beginning of knowledge; fools despise wisdom and instruction." Proverbs 1:7

My mission at Wisdom Healthcare Solutions was to provide quality home care. Once I started the business and began to advertise, I secured my first client. I'll never forget the excitement! I felt accomplished and I knew that I was on the right path. I did not care about the hefty task at hand.

Ironically, my first client was a woman who needed someone to take care of her dog – to walk it, feed it, play with it, and run errands on its behalf. Most people would've shied away from this or felt that it was beneath them, but I was elated to have my first customer. I wasn't focused so much on the task that was requested of me but was more so focused on providing excellent service. So, I submitted myself to the charge.

I became very acquainted with the woman, and her dog loved me. I was present each day to cater to its needs. A year later, the dog's owner underwent a medical emergency which required home care. Because I had taken such great care of her dog, she hired me. That is how I got my start. And Wisdom Healthcare Solutions has since evolved into something much greater than I could've ever imagined.

But before I got to the next level, I was once again tested. At the start of my business journey, although I was no longer in high school, I was surely challenged to understand and accept my own strengths once again. That's how it works! When life dishes a lesson and you have not conquered it, the same lesson will repeat itself until you finally get it.

When I began Wisdom Healthcare Solutions, I was not confident in my ability to lead its operations. I felt that I knew nursing but not very much about running a business. I did not have a business mentor and hadn't thought of obtaining one. Soon after, I met a woman who was much more experienced in business. She was seasoned; she had been in business in a similar industry for thirty years. I thought that my knowledge of healthcare paired with her knowledge of business operations could be a great match for partnership, and she agreed. We began the journey together and things were looking up, so I thought. However, instead, I later discovered that I had made a costly mistake by partnering with her. A $50,000 one.

My business partner had other businesses, and it was revealed that those other businesses were reaping the benefits of our entity. She mismanaged funds and did not pay our business taxes. This broke my heart. Not only was I angry and frustrated with her, but I was also disappointed in myself for putting so much trust in a person that I barely knew. I was so fearful of failing that I had put myself and my livelihood in a precarious position. Wisdom was the purpose of my life that God had assigned to me, not her. I had to own my decision and pay the consequences.

As a business owner, you must be willing to have tough conversations. I understood that I needed to face what had happened head on; I needed to address the situation. I had to confront my business partner. But I also feared confrontation. Even the thought of facing her made me feel nauseous. What would I say? How would I say it? What questions should I ask her, if any? How was she going to respond? These were some of the questions I pondered. Then I mustered up the courage to have the conversation. Delaying uncomfortable conversations could ultimately destroy communication and relationships. A wound was open, and I had yet to apply pressure to stop the bleeding. Allowing any additional time to pass would've further exacerbated the conditions. So, I confronted her.

I requested a meeting with my business partner to discuss my findings. We needed to address the status of the business and our partnership moving forward. I didn't point the finger or play the blame game. I stuck to the facts as if I were an attorney, using the books and numbers as my witnesses. She could not deny the mistakes she had made. From that point, we could only look to resolve the discretion. Quickly.

***

Business partnerships are serious business. The decision to enter into one should not be taken lightly. They are almost like marriages, except more involved. You'll be intertwining personal, professional, and financial responsibilities into one. Because you'll be striving to create momentum in your business to ensure its success, you're likely to spend more time with your business partner than your loved ones.

A recent article in Harvard Business Review suggests 10 questions you should ask a potential business partner during the courting stages to determine if the partnership will be a good fit for you and your business:

1. Before entertaining a business partnership with anyone, take a deep dive into you and

your business potential partner's motives for being in business. Ask the question: "*Do we want the same things?*" Are the things you most want aligned? What differences exist? And of the things that you both desire, how much do you want and how much time, money, etc. is each of you willing to sacrifice to get it?

2. Jointly discuss when and how work will be completed. We all lead different lives, have our own work ethics, and manners in which we like to tackle tasks. It's imperative to set expectations. Ask the question: "*How hard are we going to work?*"

3. Come to terms that all contributions matter, not one partner's undertakings should be considered more significant than over the other's. Creating and honoring expectations around roles and responsibilities and having them in writing will help to avoid tension. Ask: *"How will we value contributions?"*

4. Decide when a critical business decision must be made, and you and your partner have opposing views, who will make the final call. Although such situations tend to occur in the latter stages in business, it is imperative that you and your partner create this protocol early on. *"How will we make tough decisions?"*

5. *"How will we handle conflict?"* Not everyone handles conflict the same. We all come from diverse backgrounds and experiences that help shape our perspectives and conflict resolution styles. You and your partner must find common ground between you to ensure that you both are heard and that conflicts are resolved in a timely manner.

6. What is your business strategy for ensuring objectives are met? Do you and your partner agree on the way forward, the path that will help you maximize time, effort, money, and skills? If not, how will you

arrive at consensus? Ask the question: *"What's the plan?"*

7. Equity and equality are not one in the same. In a partnership, inequalities between you and your partner will exist in some shape or form. You must be honest with one another and gain an understanding of each other's worlds and seek to understand and respect them. Asking *"where's the inequality"* can help avoid future power struggles.

8. When it comes to difficult conversations, the topic of money is right up there with politics and religion. In your partnership, *"Who gets what?"* Compensation is a tricky subject that will not only impact the partners but their families. And family members will want to weigh in. How much compensation and shares will each of you receive? Are you both in agreement?

9. Put everything in writing and make it equally accessible. Any and all company terms and

agreements should be documented and signed. Doing so will leave no room for personal interpretation should a dispute arise, and it helps to maintain clarity in the partnership. Ask: *"How will we keep track?"*

10. The eventual dissolution of your partnership is inevitable. Individual missions change, buy-outs happen, and death escapes none of us. What protocols will you put in place to avoid major legal battles in the future? Whether the partnership fails or is uber successful, *"How will it end?"*

***

In 2009, the partnership I had formed for Wisdom Healthcare Solutions ended. I learned to address areas of concern immediately, not allowing them to linger and create a domino effect. And the lesson that God revealed to me through it all is that I needed to overcome the fears that caused me to uphold people in such high regard. I was setting myself up for disappointment by doing so. They would never live up to my standards or my expectations because they simply weren't rooted in reality. I am learning to accept people as they are, as Jesus sees each of us. One of my greatest lessons was to stay in tune with the Holy Spirit, which offers us hunches that we sometimes ignore. When we go in a different direction than what God has instructed us, we learn the hard way.

Prioritizing Family

"Every wise woman buildeth her house; but the foolish plucketh it down with her hands." Proverbs 14:1

God doesn't intend for us to choose between business and family. Your business is not just for you, but it is a gift for your family also. Family should always come first. Find ways to include your spouse and your children in your vision. I was blessed that Charles and I could work together; I as the CEO and he as the COO. Even if this is not the business dynamic that best suits your situation, there are still ways to include your spouse.

When you travel, invite your spouse to tag along. Consider arriving a day before conferences begin and leaving a day or so after. This will enable you and your spouse to spend quality time together and it won't seem as though you are always away from home spending time on business activities.

Find ways to include your children and their capabilities into the business's framework. What are their strengths and interests? Provide opportunities for them to learn the business and grow with you. Send them to trainings and events where they can represent the company. Charles and I initially thought that our daughters weren't interested in joining our company, but nothing could've been further from the truth. We realized that they were just waiting for us to provide opportunities that would enable them to capitalize off their strengths and interests.

Growing a business or pursuing your dreams can give you false indication you will have time once you reach your goal. I am learning that reaching a goal is a continuous process and the family God has given me is – and should be – a part of this process.

We are all given an unknown amount of time here on earth, but we tend to live it like we have infinite days. We do not. You've never heard anyone on their

Prioritizing Family

deathbed mention that they wish they had generated $5M. You more so hear them say that they wish they had spent more time with family.

***

Prioritizing family is a concept that many business owners struggle with. After all, whether their business is doing well or operating poorly, most business owners either want to capitalize on their successes and growth by spending more time working on their business or spend time working long hours in their businesses to help make improvements. The key is to determine what will work well for you and your family structure. Here are some simple ways to set boundaries and prioritize your family:

1. Leave work at work. Schedule work time and family time separately within your schedule. When your schedule calls for work, remind your family and other important people in your life that these hours have been set aside for work. Put emergency procedures in place and ensure that everyone knows the plan. Stand

firm. Don't allow distractions during this time. This way, you are teaching others to respect your business and the rules you've established to delineate work time from family time. Once this becomes a habit, those closest to you will become accustomed to allowing you to have undisturbed work time. You'll avoid the guilt trips associated with turning people away each time they feel they want to disturb you. You'll also avoid the feeling of self-reproach that often follows when you allow such distractions instead of completing important tasks.

2. When you are with your family, be present with them. Whether you're on a scheduled family vacation or simply returning home from a day at the office, unplug. Just as you set aside time to conduct business in your day or week, you can schedule sacred family time. This is a time to shut off devices, put your work bag and laptop in a dedicated space out of sight, and connect

with your family. Merely being physically present is not enough; engage with them.

3. Schedule check-in calls with those loved ones who do not live in your household. When's the last time you checked on your parents? Your best friend? Your favorite aunt? When you routinely check in on these family members, they will know when to expect to hear from you and you will neither have to experience the guilt associated with not calling them enough, nor will you hear that constant reminder from them.

Avoiding Burnout

"How much better to get wisdom than gold! To get understanding is to be chosen rather than silver." Proverbs 16:16

By the end of 2015, Wisdom Healthcare Solutions had experienced exponential growth. Not only did we offer in-home senior care, but we also provided consulting and teaching for those looking to obtain their in-home healthcare licenses through the State of North Carolina. We started an academy for in-home care professionals.

Business seems glamourous and profitable for people who are on the outside looking in, but the tasks that kept the business afloat had become daunting. There didn't seem to be enough time in the day to get it all done, and the promise I had made to myself to carve out time to rest had become a distant memory.

Because I was in it and doing most of the work, I became burnt out and at my wits end. I was tired spiritually and emotionally and considered throwing in the towel.

One Valentine's Day, Charles and I purchased tickets well in advance to attend a church event. As the time drew near, we had decided that we could not make it and attempted to give the tickets to close friends of ours. After connecting with five different couples who said they had already made plans, we decided to put the work aside for one night. We got all dressed up and attended the event. When we arrived, I was seated next to a gentleman who began to speak to me. I initially thought that the conversation would end with after a few pleasantries, but he continued speaking to me all night. As I began to listen intently to what he had to share, I soon realized that he was ministering to me. It was as if God had provided him a roadmap into my psyche and the emotional turmoil that had been burdening me for quite some time. He somehow knew that I was in what I referred to as *Burnt*

Out City and was rapidly headed for *I Give Up Town*. Although I couldn't find the words to describe it all, he mirrored them for me. That's when I knew that our attendance at the event was orchestrated by divine design. As we continued our in-depth discussion, he revealed that he was a business development consultant who understood my pain and struggles because he was once in my shoes. He had supported countless other business owners who were once experiencing the same challenges. He suggested that I read a book called, *The E Myth*.

***

Burnout goes beyond simple fatigue. It is the emotional, physical, and mental exhaustion that occurs when stress is not managed in a timely, healthy manner. It is characterized by motivational decline and can manifest as a sense of defeat and failure. Burnout not only affects the individual who is experiencing it, but it also impacts personal and professional relationships.

As a business owner, at times you'll feel as though you can conquer any and every task. After all, the last thing we want is for our business to fail. So, we may try to do everything ourselves and not take account of the initial symptoms of burnout that God is presenting to us. Some of us just continue burning our candles at both ends and hope that relief will come soon. This is not a proactive approach.

Have you ever been so exhausted to the point that you felt that completion of even the simplest tasks seemed far-reaching? How about enduring so much stress that you begin to have frequent headaches and mood swings? Can't sleep at night? You may be experiencing burnout.

While it is important to check in with your medical professionals for strategies to help manage the symptoms of burnout or any other underlying diagnoses, there are ways to prevent it from occurring in your life. And if you do begin to feel overwhelmed, you can stop the symptoms from overtaking you.

A wise business owner is self-aware and proactive. Know thyself! And learn to know who you are before you go into business. If you know that you have control and trust issues that have previously prevented you from delegating tasks, whether those tasks were personal or professional, put structures into place to prevent this from causing you to become overwhelmed and hindering your business in the future.

Structures are key to any successful business. Everything from time to customer management requires structure. It's what helps us as busy business owners to be productive and organized. A lack of productivity and organization could cause you to feel as though you're spinning your wheels, unable to clearly gauge the small wins, and clouding the next steps toward the goals you've identified.

Frequent check-ins with your identified allies – teammates, mentors, advisors, therapists, physicians, close family and friends – are essential. If you have the type of personality that prevents you from contacting others because you "don't want to bother anyone," form a check-in system that enables contact on a consistent basis, even when things are going well.

This way, if you're having a lousy day, month, or quarter, and you are beginning to feel overwhelmed, your support system is aware and can step in with a helping hand, offer methods that have helped them get through tough times, or share fresh ideas.

Finally, be mindful. Live in the present moment. Use methods such as prayer and meditation to help regulate your mind, body, and spirit. The answers that you need will often be right in front of you. To access them, you'll just have to quiet your mind and calm your spirit. This is a practice that should also be regularly incorporated into your proactive toolkit. It will help you remember to address the one or two things that you can do right at each moment of the day to improve your situation.

Scaling

"Oh, the depth of the riches and wisdom and knowledge of God! How unsearchable are His judgments and how inscrutable His ways." Romans 11: 33-35

Growth is exciting. It means your business idea is working. You're attracting customers, making sales, and gaining traction. But here's the thing: growth and scaling aren't the same. Growth adds revenue by adding resources. Scaling adds revenue *without* a significant increase in costs.

Scaling is what takes you from a successful small operation to a sustainable, well-oiled machine that can handle ten times the demand without ten times the chaos. It's about leveraging efficient processes. Through automating these processes and leveraging your existing resources, scaling becomes more sustainable.

Not every business is set up to scale and not everyone even wants to scale their business. Believe it or not, scaling too soon could hurt your business. Before you decide, you must revisit your why and create another clear vision and strategy. This will help you to escape avoidable challenges in the long haul. Consider the following when creating your growth strategy:

1. Do you have the right team in place?
2. Is the technology that you use to perform business tasks sufficient?
3. What is your plan to acquire and retain more customers?
4. Once you acquire more customers, are your processes and procedures efficient enough to maintain excellent customer service?

When businesses scale without a plan, the results could prove detrimental to their continued success. Some businesses struggle with maintaining

Scaling

high standards and high-quality products, while others find it difficult to maintain a quality workforce. Instead of hiring competent staff, they begin hiring under-qualified workers just to meet customer demand. Sometimes owners want to scale but they are not amenable to changing how they do business, despite rapidly changing industries and processes in an ever-changing world. Others find it difficult to maintain their brand identity altogether.

***

I was contemplating purchasing the book *The E Myth* as the gentleman had suggested. The day that I spoke to him at our church event was a Friday. I couldn't get our conversation out of my head, but I allowed my responsibilities and other distractions to halt my desire to move forward and purchase the book.

By Monday, to my surprise, the gentleman I had met and recommended the book personally showed up to my office. He smiled and handed me a copy of the book. All excuses and barriers, removed.

I began reading the book right away, only to become upset by it. Did I really give the illusion of a schizophrenic person? Is that how I was presenting to those around me? Did I truly come across as someone who did not know what she was doing and seemed to have hands in too many pots? However, I continued reading until the end. The knowledge that I gained was invaluable. I discovered that there are two ways to scale a business.

The first method for scaling a business is to open several offices and hire office managers. Many law firms and doctors' offices scale using this model. Some of the benefits of opening several offices and hiring strong office managers is that it removes the business owners from managing the day-to-day activities of the business so they can focus on strategic partnerships and growth. However, this model could prove to be very costly, as the business would be responsible for owning or leasing office space, funding all its operations across locations, and staffing gifts and woes.

Scaling

The second method for scaling a business is to create a franchise model. Franchising is when an established company offers their brand – their name, model, and systems – for other businesses to operate under. A franchisor and franchisee relationship is formed; the franchisor earns royalties and fees in exchange. Many successful brands from various industries such as fast-food restaurants, like Chick-Fila, urgent medical care services, like Patient First, hardware stores, like ACE Hardware, and fitness gyms, such as Planet Fitness, use a franchising model.

The franchising model works by enabling business owners to become *franchisees* by establishing a business that will operate under a brand that has developed a proven system. The established business that has created that system – the *franchisor* – is afforded the opportunity to expand without managing each location. This form of scaling intrigued me the most.

I discussed the possibilities with my husband, Charles. Immediately, he began researching franchise models and educational opportunities. Based on the research, we decided that franchising was the best way to scale our business, and we filed a franchise disclosure document with the Federal Trade Commission (FTC) as Wisdom Senior Care. Charles also stumbled upon information on the International Franchise Association.

Founded in 1960, The International Franchise Association, or IFA, is a nonprofit organization that was founded in 1960. The main mission of the organization is to promote, enhance, and protect franchising through the advocacy and support of its members. The organization is currently headquartered in Washington, D.C. and represents more than 1,400 brands and 600 supplier businesses globally.

After consideration, Charles and I decided to attend the IFA's annual conference which took place during the month of February 2016 in Arizona. The president of the organization at that time was Robert Cresenti, a very humble, open man. Charles and I approached Robert to ask questions. Instead of answering them all, he invited us to sit in on one of the organization's closed board meetings. This invitation was unheard of! People kept coming up to us afterwards asking how we knew Robert Cresenti, but the truth was we had just met.

We enrolled as active IFA members that year. I joined several committees within its membership and in 2019 was elected to the board of directors. My role on board was to represent smaller, emerging brands. To this day, I continue to bring small brands to the table.

By reflecting on my journey, I am reminded that sometimes we're looking for something outside of ourselves or our environment to solve our problems. The man I had met at the Valentine's Day event had been a member of our church for years. He watched our children grow up.

Discovering Wisdom Today

"Everyone who hears these words of mine and does them will be like a wise man who built his house on the rock."
Matthew 7:24

Today, Wisdom Senior Care continues to stand strong in its commitment to provide quality, compassionate care for seniors in the comfort of their own homes. We offer companionship and assistance with daily living activities such as personal care and medication management. Our caregivers undergo an extensive background check process and training to ensure they are aligned with our company's mission, values, and standard of excellence.

We are an award-winning franchise that is rapidly expanding across the United States, with current franchisees that have very strong footprints in North Carolina, South Carolina, and Florida. Our franchisees receive our unwavering support to ensure their success. And some of our franchisees operate multiple locations.

When I started this business, I had no idea how big God's vision was. It certainly outweighed my own, but with His help, we have been able to achieve the most inconceivable accomplishments.

I attribute our success to each and every franchisee and team member who wakes up each day prepared to provide our customers with the best care possible. I attribute it to our back-office team that strives to ensure we are operating a business of integrity and innovation. I also attribute it to my wonderful family who have made sacrifices and have shown their unwavering commitment from the very beginning.

Have you considered beginning an in-home senior care business? Consider joining the remarkable team at Wisdom Senior Care. You'll have access to our top tier brand and blueprint; we'll help you with the rest.

Visit our website at wisdomseniorcare.com for more information.

Forgiving

"But the wisdom that comes from heaven is first of all pure; then peace-loving, considerate, submissive, full of mercy and good fruit, impartial and sincere." James 3:17

Through the trials, disappointments, backstabbing, the difficult days and sleepless nights, the envy and hate, the doubt, fears, and failures, successful business owners don't give up. This is what sets them apart. But to achieve success and to be genuinely happy, it is my belief that we must learn to forgive. We must learn to let go and forgive often.

Forgiveness is a kindness to yourself. That's right; it is for you. It is a conscious decision to move forward without malice, regret, or condemnation. It is a release of the anger, hurt, guilt, and feelings of betrayal that we come to realize are not serving our purpose. It is accepting that there are lessons in failure and embracing those lessons to become better human beings.

In a biblical sense, forgiveness is God's promise not to count our sins against us once we repent. Repentance involves turning away from our sins and having faith in the Almighty. And in Christianity, God's forgiveness of us lies in our willingness to forgive others, including ourselves.

***

Have you heard the saying I will forgive you, but I will not forget? I have learned that to truly forgive means to forget what happened. This does not mean that you are not aware of the experiences that have gotten you off track, but it means that you are willing to let go and move on without giving them any additional mental, emotional, or spiritual energy that is causing you and others harm.

I firmly believe that the success I've experienced in business is a direct result of forgiveness. The more I have forgiven others for their shortcomings, forgiven

Forgiving

myself for my own transgressions. The more I ask God for forgiveness, the more I have prospered. When we let go, we position ourselves to receive greater.

I now understand that it is God who provides the opportunity for me to do what I am doing. He is the CEO of all that I do. I humbly turn to God in prayer before I make any decisions. This submission helps me to stop the comparison game and to operate in my purpose with all integrity and love for myself, my clients, and my business. Some may think that this seems cliché; but to pray, listen, and move forward on what God states requires a lot of courage.

Acknowledgements

I would like to express my deepest gratitude to my beloved husband, Charles, for his unwavering support and patience. To my wonderful children, Jasmine and Moriah, and my grandchildren, Jayden and Ayanna, always pursue the passion in your heart. I appreciate my siblings, Angela, Tracey, and Grady, and my aunt, Cheryl, for always having a listening ear. I appreciate the countless hours you've spent with me, offering your thoughtful encouragement and constant reminders of God's steadfast presence during my most challenging times.

About the Author

With twenty years of nursing and home healthcare experience in the Triangle area, Carolyn Thurston started Wisdom Senior Care in 2006. With the support of her team, she has grown Wisdom Senior Care with the mission to keep more of our seniors happy at home by focusing on improvements to promote optimal senior care and change the perception of aging. Her advocacy for providing health care for seniors and improving the quality of care for them in their home setting, changing the perception of aging, leading changes in the senior in-home care industry, and successfully facilitating health care initiatives allows her to manage operational performance and strengthen Wisdom Senior Care's franchise brand growth while prioritizing on diversity and inclusion.

Serving others was instilled in Carolyn as a young child by her father who served in the military. This left an indelible mark that became the driving force that cultivated her to become the Founder and Chief Executive Officer of Wisdom Senior Care. Having an opportunity to travel with her father all over the world, she gravitated to being of service to seniors. With that passion ignited from her youth, she focused her efforts and pursued studying in the field of Health Care and Sociology at North Carolina Central University in which she graduated with a Bachelor of Arts in Sociology. In addition, Carolyn continued her education at Winston Salem State University and graduated with a Bachelor of Science in Nursing with honors.

Carolyn is an active industry spokesperson in healthcare and in the business community. She has

About the Author

been nationally recognized for her expertise in the field, for her positive impact and leading the industry with several recognitions. She was honored with The Franchise Action Network (2019) award, an award given to people who work tirelessly to protect, promote, and enhance the franchise industry. She works hard with lawmakers on the Capitol to promote healthy policies for a healthy business environment.

Carolyn was recognized with The Women's Business Center Award (2019) for providing business opportunities through franchising. She now serves on the International Franchise Association Board of Directors and Vice Chair of the Black Franchise Leadership Council.

Carolyn places emphasis on the importance of technology in providing in-house data for business owners' ability to make data- driven decisions and the role that AR and VR in preventing and assisting seniors living with Alzheimer's & Dementia. She also focuses a significant amount of time on fostering relationships and providing academic programs through Wisdom

Health Academy to expand the capability and capacity of the healthcare field to meet the current and future needs of the aging population. She is highly active with Wisdom Missions Worldwide, a non-profit with the highest ambition to bring assistance to skilled experts (caregivers) who struggle with burn out in their calling to serve seniors and underserved seniors who experience abuse, by increasing their accessibility to quality services.

References

Bhasin, K. (2023, August 18). *4 Gigantic Companies That Started From Nothing.* American Express. Retrieved from https://www.americanexpress.com/en-us/business/trends-and-insights/articles/4-gigantic-companies-that-started-from-nothing/

Black, M. and Tarver, J. (2022, May 9). *8 Small Business Financing Options: Get The Funding You Need.* Forbes. Retrieved from https://www.forbes.com/advisor/business-loans/business-funding/

Boekem, B. (2024, May 13). *What Makes A Good Business Partnership?* Forbes. Retrieved from https://www.forbes.com/councils/forbestechcouncil/2024/05/13/what-makes-a-good-business-partnership/

Fagan, A. (2018, March 1). *What Does It Mean to Be Wise?* Psychology Today. Retrieved from https://www.psychologytoday.com/us/blog/between-cultures/201803/what-does-it-mean-to-be-wise?msockid=2f829924475361c702298abf462160ed

International Franchise Association. *About IFA.* Retrieved from https://www.franchise.org/about-us/

Smith, T. (2025, July 25). *Crowdfunding: What It Is, How It Works, and Popular Websites*. Investopedia. Retrieved from https://www.investopedia.com/terms/c/crowdfunding.asp

U.S Small Business Administration. (2025, March 7). *Choose a Business Structure*. Retrieved from https://www.sba.gov/business-guide/launch-your-business/choose-business-structure

Zucker, R. and Becker. (2023, August 18). *Questions to Ask Before Entering a Business Partnership.* Harvard Business Review. Retrieved from https://hbr.org/2023/08/10-questions-to-ask-before-entering-a-business-partnership

www.ingramcontent.com/pod-product-compliance
Lightning Source LLC
Chambersburg PA
CBHW050914160426
43194CB00011B/2401